I CAN LEAD?

Overcoming something today to lead better tomorrow

SPENCER ROSS

Contents

Chapter 1

Serve

"Life's most persistent and urgent question is, 'What are you doing for others?'"

– Martin Luther King Jr.

A good leader serves those around them. What do you see when you look around? What associations do you make with your observations? Maybe you are at your desk at work, maybe at home, or at your kids' game. Is there someone around you who would benefit from an encouraging smile or friendly greeting? Perhaps you see the trash needs to be taken out. Someone might need guidance on a project or someone to sit with them at lunch. There's opportunity everywhere you look. The reality is that we all like being noticed to a certain degree, to be at least acknowledged, and to be treated well. I remember my mom would put flowers in the bathrooms at church. Everyone would talk about the flowers. Adding some color to the bathroom is such a simple thing. But, something so simple made everyone's day brighter. That is the power leaders have. No one ever told her to put the flowers there; she did it because she saw a need, thought about it, and filled it. Everyone noticed the action and felt the results.

Doing the little things without being told and helping out demonstrates care for others and your environment. The Boy Scouts and Girl Scouts have the slogan "Do a good turn daily." Why? Helping others is impactful. Leaders look around and see what they can improve, what needs to be done, and who needs help. They understand that it is the action, big or small, that can have an impact towards the result they want. Contrarily, followers wait for someone else to do what they see needs to be done or be told to help. Sometimes that means you will help people, and no one will notice or maybe someone else will even take the credit. But, you have to look at your motivation.

CEOs often claim that they are there to serve their employees. This also can be seen in mottos of organizations around the world. The Los Angeles Police Department motto is "To Protect and to Serve." The Chinese Army's (People's Liberation Army) motto is "Serve the People." Think of a good leader you've had in your life. Chances are, that person served well. Good leadership is marked by good service. If you want to be a great leader, look around you and start helping others. Not only will you improve your ability to lead others, you might also inspire others to help as well. My mom was an example for me on how to serve others. I saw how she acted and it made me think. She was paying attention to the details and taking notice of what could be done to improve the environment.

Another way to serve others is by helping the person in charge. I listened to a Rapid Response episode on the Masters of

Scale with Reid Hoffman Podcast called Winning and losing w/ Vanderbilt University coach, Jerry Stackhouse. Coach Stackhouse talked about helping the helper during the game. He talked about critiquing his players after the game about not helping someone who is helping someone else or who has the ball. It was the best way I have ever heard it said. What are you doing off the ball (not in charge)? What about when someone is in charge, and he's talking to the team leads (your boss). What are you going to do?

In team sports, a couple of people can dominate the game, but two people can't win a basketball game by themselves. Just as with sports- business, community, and life are the same way.

There is a story about President Franklin Roosevelt visiting troops at the hospital. He was a leader by title, but he knew he could inspire just as much with his actions and words as well as how he presented himself.

When he would meet the general public or have pictures taken of him, he would not have his wheelchair in view because he wanted to look strong. He understood that leaders must project power, so he made sure to visually show that he was strong even if it was inconvenient and took longer to make the presentation.

When he went to a military hospital to thank the service members for their service during World War II, he was pushed around in his wheelchair, laughing and making sure everyone knew he was there. He was so careful to portray an image of strength at other times, but at the military hospitals, he knew he could inspire. He used his own story to serve others and demonstrated value in spite of his perceived disability.

We can all imagine that seeing the President of the United States in a wheelchair gave a bold message. Being in a wheelchair didn't hold him back from the presidency. He went to the hospital as a person in a wheelchair to inspire others to be greater. It can be discouraging to be in a hospital or to be hurt. He didn't have to go there and talk to people, but he knew what would help them be encouraged and how to lift them up, so he did. He served them by sharing his story.

There are some questions you can reflect on as you're practicing service leadership:

Is what I am doing supporting people, or am I just doing something because it makes me feel good?

Am I making a thought-out effort to serve, or am I just randomly helping?

What is the result of me serving?

Chapter 2

Attitude

"The Swedes will go on beating us for a long time, but eventually they will teach us how to beat them." – Peter the Great

Many people say that attitude is everything. I don't know if it's everything, but it is very important. Attitude is what you are thinking or feeling. I know I am more efficient when I am positive about the task. An attitude can be infectious in a positive or negative way and can influence others. A negative attitude can be like a cancer that eats strength away. If the attitude is positive, it can be that ray of light that makes the work finish quicker. You can be a positive influence, even a leader, through your attitude.

Have a positive attitude. It is infectious. There is a saying, "more things are caught than taught." People observe the way we interact with others. Give a pleasant "yes" when you're asked to do something. Make positive connections with others through greeting them. (Even the people who you don't like!) Ask people how they're doing and really listen to their response. Others will see this and will be inspired to be positive as well. This is one way you can lead your environment without even talking about leadership.

Be a leader in the lives of those around you by recognizing the power your response has. You are responsible for your actions and how you respond; you dictate your own actions. If someone wrongs you, you can be a leader in the way you react. Don't lash out. Instead, think of how you can lead through your response. You can shock them by remaining respectful and keeping a positive attitude in the midst of conflict.

Your body language says a lot about you and how you perceive the people you're around: look people in the eyes, shake their hand, smile at them, stand with your body towards them. Arms… you can't chop them off, so you have to do something with them. Whatever makes you comfortable, do that. Some people have said not to cross your arms, as it can make you look defensive. But if that's how you feel most comfortable in a conversation, don't sweat it. Do what works for you. If having your arms at your side is what you like, then do that. I like putting my arms across my chest, which is a slight deviation from crossing them. I also talk with my hands. I point, wave, motion, and do all sorts of things, but I know some people get distracted so I try to limit it. At the same time, be authentic to yourself, your situation, and your audience. If your body language makes people think you are uninterested in what they have to say, then you are losing your ability to influence them.

German Chancellor, Angela Merkel, holds her hands in a very specific way. Maybe she was intentional about it, or maybe it just happened. Either way, people have remembered it. Her political party has used it to promote her. Some people have called it the Triangle of Power or Merkel Diamond. Sounds cool, right? Merkel demonstrates her interest in the conversation, while also maintaining her own comfort. Be comfortable with how you carry yourself. Remember, as a leader, your perceived body language impacts those around you.

Oftentimes, the attitude of a group is referred to as the group culture. What is your group culture? If your attitude is positive or negative, then that can change the culture of the group. Your impact on the world, or people around you, is in large part under your control. Others and outside events will influence you and your reputation, but you get to decide what you do. Consider how you can influence the group culture of a team you're on. Everything you do and say can have an impact. It might take a long time of being friendly, smiling, talking with people to influence others, but do not give up. There will always be that one person who is negative; you do not have to be the negative one. It does not mean you have to be a cheerleader, but find your own way to be positive. If you have an attitude of finding the positive, it will encourage others to be positive.

You are responsible for your attitude. Lead yourself. What is your mindset? How are you making your own personal culture a positive one? Your attitude will be seen and heard by those around you. Your attitude will influence those around you and start to create a culture. Take control of your environment by taking control of your attitude.

Thoughts?

Is my tone and body language saying I feel _____?

If so, am I dumping my _______ on people and not being responsible/considerate in my interactions?

How can I improve my attitude?

Chapter 3
Work hard

"Peace is a daily, weekly, a monthly process, gradually changing opinions, slowly eroding old barriers, quietly building new structures."
– John F. Kennedy

Being a leader takes work. Everyone works, right? So does that mean everyone is a leader? Not necessarily. Working hard doesn't mean you are a leader, but a leader will work hard no matter who gets the credit. Being a good leader takes a lot of work. Anyone can do something once, but it's hard to be consistent and leading is a mindset. Show you can lead by how you do the job.

I got out of the Navy and went to Basic Training for the Army in 2019. Graduation day happened to be on Thanksgiving, so some friends and I went out for breakfast. We had the rest of the day off, so we found a homeless dinner to volunteer at. We were very early, so we offered to help set the place up. They said they didn't need any help as most of the setup was done, thanked us for our service, and told us to relax. After sitting around for about 30 minutes, we noticed the floor was dirty. We moved all the furniture, swept, vacuumed, mopped, reset the tables and chairs, wiped everything down, put the silverware back out, cleaned the kitchen, and cleaned the bathroom. We split up cleaning the bathroom, so it wasn't one guy cleaning the entire thing. The two people who were running the shelter were brought to tears when they saw everything we did. We also felt fulfilled knowing that we were able to make the shelter a better place for everyone. Working hard looks different depending on what you are doing, but hard work is always valuable.

As a person, you will be criticized. Someone won't like your idea. Someone will say you are worthless and stupid. You will go for a loan, present a project, go for a job interview, have a manuscript for a movie or play, ask for training, ask for a raise, ask for a raise for someone on your team, and not get it because of whatever excuse they make up. It will take internal fortitude to keep going and be nice. It is hard when people are not as nice as you think they should be or do or say something you disagree with. Did you ask someone out, and they said no? Keep being nice and engage them, and that doesn't mean keep asking them out. It is hard to be told no and not retaliate or respond in a disrespectful way. Learn how to leverage experiences that don't go your way for your own growth.

The movie, Bowling for Columbine by Michael Moore is about the school shooting at Columbine High School. After the shooting, people were asking lots of questions, and many people were saying and blaming lots of different people, music, culture, and things. Moore interviewed Marilyn Manson and asked him, "If you were to talk directly to the kids at Columbine or the people in that community, what would you say to them if they were here right now?" (I shortened the question for brevity.) As Moore finished his question, I thought of a few things I would say. Manson's response blew me away, "I wouldn't say a single word to them. I would listen to what they would have to say, and that's what no one did." Profound. He was right. It is so easy to talk and say what is on your mind. It is hard, very hard, to listen to someone, especially when you don't like what they're saying. But don't worry, listening is a skill you can develop. Asking the right questions is good sometimes, but sometimes not asking anything and just being there to listen to what someone has to say is more important. Sometimes, and I have learned this through many errors, all you can do is just be there and let them express how they feel. Listening is another form of hard work that will develop your ability to lead. Good leaders listen well.

Sometimes hard work looks like having hard conversations. Don't send an email with your complaint. Call the person on the phone, or better yet, go have a meeting in person. Yes, you are busy, but so are they. Waiting is not going to make it easier so don't be lazy. Take the time to do the hard thing and look him in the eye when you are having a complicated conversation.

I had a boss named Ray Blackwell. He called me on the phone or would drive down to the school where I worked to tell me or someone else bad news or have the hard conversation. There is a time and place for email, text, or written documentation, but are you using it as the easy way out? It is easy to misinterpret someone's tone in an email. It is hard to mentor someone over an email. It can be done, but it is easier to misinterpret what you mean in an email; it can be impersonal, and it is harder to mentor someone by email. I can't tell you the great mentorship I would get from Ray by him correcting me on an issue, asking me why I did something, and then working through what I should have done for the next time. He was trying to set me up for success the next time the same issue would come around. He wanted me to be an independent problem-solver, and that is difficult to convey via email. Do the hard thing by choosing the right way to have conversations.

Other times, hard work looks like biting your tongue. If you have a negative interaction with someone, take a moment and think; then, talk to them like you would want someone to talk to you. It is hard being nice to the people who we disagree with or are having issues with. It is very hard to lead people who are not nice, can't plan correctly, can't communicate clearly or communicate at all, and are accusatory. But, not reacting negatively to this behavior is part of being a good leader. If you feel like you can't respond well, pause and continue when you are ready.

Hard work isn't always physically demanding. Sometimes, hard work looks like being in the locker room after a national tragedy and telling your friends it will be ok. Hard work also might look like hugging someone, listening, offering clothes, providing moving boxes or just listening. Lean in to what your environment needs. They need your leadership, even when it is hard.

Chapter 4

Take responsibility

"In the long run, we shape our lives, and we shape ourselves. The process never ends until we die. And the choices we make are ultimately our own responsibility." – Eleanor Roosevelt

Responsibility is taking credit and or ownership. Taking responsibility for the good and bad is a quality of a leader. It's always easy to take credit for positive outcomes, but being a leader means you also own the negative outcomes.

Leaders have to make the hard decisions. These decisions can be about social security, budgetary issues, feelings, good and bad ideas, and people's pet projects. Some leadership decisions impact others' lives in huge ways, so it's the job of the leader to consider all possible outcomes and involve necessary people to discuss, consider, and make conclusions. For peace treaties, discipline, moderating political debates, whether Presidential debates to the PTA or HOA board meeting and everything in between, who is going to ask the hard questions? Who is going to create an environment where people feel comfortable asking questions? Who is going to bring the different people or opposing sides together? The leader.

There are some people with whom you will not get along with. It might be their voice, mannerisms, conduct, beliefs, or how they treat you. Whatever it is, get over it! A good leader doesn't let that stand in the way of being at peace with everyone as much as possible. Keep reaching out. Keep engaging. Keep being nice. Martin Luther King Jr. talked about if you're not at the meeting, you don't have a voice. If you don't engage with the person, you can't be a positive influence in their life.

My friend, Alexis, was a waitress. One of Alexis' coworkers was mean to everyone. This coworker was older than Alexis and worked at the company longer than most. But Alexis didn't let this stop her from being a leader. Alexis said it took her a year of being super nice to her coworker to get her to start to change her mean behavior. That's a long time and a lot of dedication and courage. There were days when she was physically or mentally tired, and frustrated with her situation. Sometimes she didn't respond to her coworker the best way, so she'd go back and make it right. But she kept trying and turned someone who was not a friend of anyone into a friend of everyone. She took personal ownership of the situation to make the place better. She was successful. That is good leadership.

Not only should you take care to build up those around you, but you should take care to build up yourself. Is someone going to give you a job, or are you going to have to work hard for it? Various opportunities will present themselves in your life, but you have to take ownership of the opportunities. I have a friend who has worked in mental health for over 30 years. He visits people in their homes who have disabilities. He also offers support while a primary caretaker goes to run errands or take care of other responsibilities. He has been with a wide range of individuals: young and old, disabled from birth or from a life circumstance. He has been to 8 states and 23 countries, teaching about disabilities and working on medical equipment. He has taught people with doctorates, physical therapists, occupational therapists, surgeons, pharmacists, and social workers. He has worked with mentally disabled sex offenders and was one of the few men at his company to work with women. He has been punched, kicked, had stuff thrown at him, and been yelled at. He started a ministry fixing wheelchairs and goes to 3rd world countries to fix wheelchairs, talk about mental health or disabilities, and Jesus Christ. Needless to say, he is an amazing man, very smart, great to talk to, patient, and willing to help wherever he can. When I interviewed him for this book, he had me sit at his desk to work, and he sat in the visitor's seat. He did this because he thought it would be easier for me to take notes. He was right. Let's just distill all this information to: he's the guy you want in your corner. He's a supporter and a friend to all. His name is Dana Croxton. When he was six, his mom had her first mental breakdown. When he was 12, he was playing, and his dad came to him and said, "You're done. You're done playing. Give your toys away; you need to help the family." He went to school, worked at home, got a job at 15, and didn't go to parties or football games. He was an overweight and twitchy kid who wasn't "cool." He graduated high school and joined the Air Force, and when he got out, he became homeless and wandered and drank and did drugs. He has thick glasses, and he has a disability himself. He finally had enough. He became a Christian and turned his life around. Dana found a career that he enjoyed, was good at, paid the bills, and would allow him to retire one day. He has helped so many people and done so much good, but if you judged him based on what he looks like, or the fact he was homeless, did drugs, used to get drunk, or only has a high school diploma, you wouldn't think he has gone to 8 states and 23 countries to help improve the lives of thousands. Mental health is a vast field of study, and there are many opportunities to have a career in the area. He found a spot. He worked hard, learned from mistakes, taught those around him, and kept a positive attitude. He took what life had given him and made it work. He took responsibility and made the most of his opportunities.

Step into your role and take responsibility. Some people might not be happy about your position. While this will be challenging, push through and don't be fake with those people. People might be tricked by you being fake for a while, but people don't like insincerity and will figure it out. Don't enable bad behavior to increase, but gently and firmly work on the culture. Talk to the people about what is expected of them and be fair, but don't let the poison of people talking you or others down continue. Look for opportunities to encourage and praise your team. Not fake praise. It is hard to watch someone get appointed, just as it might be hard to be appointed. Take the time to grow with them and learn from your mistakes. Dana found his place in life. What is the difference between him and you?

Taking responsibility for your actions and how you end up in life might seem small, but you need this skill in order to be the leader in your life. Doing something wrong? Don't wait for someone to tell you to stop. Just stop. Someone telling you you aren't very good? Listen to what they have to say and grow, but don't listen to the people trying to hold you back. Want to be a better leader, technical expert, teacher, entrepreneur, or businesswoman? There are online classes, seminars, college courses, military, books, magazines, news articles, people who can mentor you, different jobs you can do that allow you to promote and manage more people, and so on. You are responsible for yourself and your own improvement. Want to be a better parent or spouse? There are online classes, books, and older people who have been there. You might be asking, "What does that have to do with being a better leader or responsibility?" Good leaders manage all opportunities well, including those in their homes. Don't be the best restaurant owner and forget about your family.

Some questions to reflect on taking responsibility:

What in your life can you improve?

Are you asking people to help you with your blind spots?

As you improve, are you raising up the people around you to take control of their life?

Chapter 5

But I'm not perfect or in charge

"If they can make penicillin out of moldy bread, they can sure make something out of you." – Muhammad Ali

Actions have consequences. True but we need to keep going. There will always be someone or something that is there to hold us back from being the best. We need to rise up and keep going. We need to push aside those doubts and memories to be the leader our team needs.

Bob is the boss at a large company. He tells people beneath him that he is in charge. Bob is Eric's direct boss and Bob doesn't like Eric. Bob avoids Eric and says hello to the "important" people, but not Eric or the other people beneath him. Eric frequently asks for help and feedback from Bob, but Bob ignores him. Even still, Eric is a great employee who exceeds the standards set for his role and tries to be super nice to Eric. One day, Eric got a flat tire before work. He decided not to call or text Bob because Bob just had a baby and it was very early. When Eric got to work, he realized that he was still the first employee to arrive by hours, even though he was late. He went about his morning responsibilities and then continued with his day.

A few days later, Bob called Eric into his office and pressed him about the morning he was late to work. Bob yelled at Eric, told him he was a bad worker, and had been telling other people Eric was a bad worker. Eric felt defeated because he was trying to be nice and not text early in the morning, knew he was trying his best, and had a near-perfect record. But, instead of getting visibly angry at Bob, Eric calmly identified his understanding of policy and acknowledged that he should have told Bob he was going to be late. Eric then cited the multiple instances where he's demonstrated exceptional work. In this moment, Eric owned his mistake but also took the opportunity to identify some of his strengths.

Ok, he was in a super difficult situation and he made a mistake. Did he stop being nice after he was called out for 1 thing? No. Was he in charge? No. Did he wait for someone else to come along and help him? No, he took responsibility for the situation and worked at the relationship. Did he ask for help and advice? Yes, but he didn't wait for the answer to be given to him; he went out and looked for it. He was realistic about what he thought he could accomplish and set some goals. Sometimes the goals are small, and people would pick other goals. As a leader, you need to select the goals with input from those around you that work for you. Look at all the available information and make a decision. Don't let perfect be the enemy of the good. You could wait years to make the right decision. Make a decision. Ask for advice and keep going. If everyone quit after they did something wrong, no one would ever lead.

Let's say there was a scandal in the organization where you worked. "During this time, we all need to come together. We need to overcome adversity and be resilient. We need to be proactive in how we manage ourselves. In this time, we need to build sustainable resiliency. We need to remember change is constant, and we need to embrace the opportunity. We need to refocus on what matters. There will be choppy waters ahead. We need to develop diverse talent and work hard at promoting inclusivity. We need to be bold in the next steps we take over the coming months. Forward thinking is the name of the game. We need to not lose perspective on what this company stands for. Remember that you and what you do are important. Remember that family is important and that you are family. We are here for you as we go through this trial together."

Have you heard a speech like this before? Where you or the people they are talking to have nothing to do with the issue but someone keeps saying we? Words matter. These themes are sayings that people will rely upon to bring people together and motivate them but there is a need to focus on the issue at hand. Don't clump a bunch of points or vague phrases to comfort your team or a person.

In fact, you WILL make mistakes. Sometimes you will make big mistakes, and sometimes they'll be so small that no one will know but you. If you make a mistake, don't repeat it. Just stop whatever it is. Every moment is an opportunity to be better. The best decision you can make is to not make the same mistake. You don't need to go around telling everyone about it because that will not make it better. Apologize if you can, but don't force your apology onto someone.

Don't write a speech like the one above. Whether you did something wrong or someone else did, make an authentic speech from your heart. Don't just offer professional platitudes and think that will solve your problem. Hold yourself accountable, just like you hold the people around you accountable. I realize we don't all have a mom or dad or your home might be poisonous but watch the people around you. It is a simple place to find an example. Regardless of your situation, try to find a mentor. It will take time, but they are out there, and sometimes you will need different people to help you solve different problems. Mark Twain said, "When I was a boy of 14, my father was so ignorant I could hardly stand to have the old man around. But when I got to be 21, I was astonished at how much the old man had learned in 7 years." Sometimes the person to ask for advice is your parents. Lots of people want to give you advice, but you need to make sure you are working on trying to find the right people to ask. Maybe, in learning about leadership, you read something in a book or heard a story about someone who did something to overcome a similar situation to whatever you might be facing and that helps inspire you to come up with a creative solution. Being a good leader often takes time and mentorship, and you making the effort to do the right thing.

Conversely, if you are mentoring someone, try to help them if you can, but it is not your job to save everyone. Be realistic in the goals you set. Sometimes it's the little things that build to the bigger things. You are responsible for your actions, but can only do so much to encourage others. If you find that someone you're mentoring isn't acting on any of your feedback and is stuck in a cycle, you can take a step back. Leaders often mentor others, but be cognizant of what you're willing to put up with.

You need to lead by example. Sometimes that means letting people fail. You can be a great leader who has made mistakes and grown or just another boss who abuses power. You don't need a title to do the right thing. Find a mentor to help guide you before you do the wrong thing, but after you do the wrong thing, don't give up on life, say you're sorry, and keep going.

Questions to think about:

When you talk to people, are you taking time to talk about what is important or just saying a bunch of big words?

Are you promoting a culture of cover-ups or accountability with true transparency?

Are you growing from your's and others' mistakes or using the "I'm growing" to justify stupid decisions?

Chapter 6

Humility

"If you want to go fast, go alone. If you want to go far, go together."
– African proverb

What does it mean to be humble? Some people look at humility as a weakness. However, asking for help, using a team to get things accomplished, being curious and asking questions are all traits of good leaders. And aren't we trying to lead or to be the best? Are you the example people measure themselves against? Would that make you the top company, producer, or composer? Mahammad Ali said he was the greatest. Well, other people said they were the greatest. Can you be the greatest and still be humble? It sounds like greatness can be subjective.

Did you get promoted? Congratulations! Now that you have a new job, you should be learning new things. What should you be learning now? How can you improve?

Cultivate a spirit of curiosity and keep learning. You should look to learn about new and different ways something can be done, and then teach the team. Nelson Mandela said that, "Education is the most powerful weapon which you can use to change the world."

How do you measure growth or success? Talk to someone you trust, but more education will help you get that answer. It might change now that you have a new job. If you think that you are the only one who has great ideas, check yourself. That would be an example of arrogance and a quality of a bad leader. Keep asking people about what they do, how they do it, and why.

Keep reading about different ideas. Leaders who just read about leadership and don't practice it don't have the experience to lead when things get messy. You want to be dynamic and able to handle any situation. Leaders who try to lead without studying will have a hard time thinking of different solutions to problems by themselves. You'll need to continue to invest in your growth so that you can build those muscles. Your team will see you check out new opportunities and could be inspired to do the same. As someone in charge, are you promoting the abilities of those around you and teaching them new skills? Encourage them to apply for different positions and for them to grow. Be the leader that you always wanted. Take all the good that you have learned about, and don't perpetuate the bad. Acting like you know it all after being promoted is annoying. Maybe you got there all on your own. Honestly, that is very rare. Someone somewhere helped you get to where you are today. Saying thank you to those people would be great and you could use their example and help lift others up.

Teamwork

See where you can help. Your knowledge, time, insight, hands or muscles, ability to talk to someone or hold their hand, your voice to stand up for someone, your different perspective, your ability to give the presentation or teach, or whatever you are good at might help someone. You have something to offer, and people will need your help. Some people will be too hurt or scared or too arrogant to ask for help. A leader does their best. If it was your project and you needed an extra person, would you want that person to do their best or give 50% effort? What about 90% effort, but not their best? Now you have a project or company and you have 2 employees, 50 employees, or 1000 employees. Would you want 1 employee or all your employees doing their best? Why? You work your hardest; wouldn't you expect someone who works for you to work their hardest too? Now think about being on someone's team. Even as the CEO, you are a team member. Shareholders, employees, customers, bankers who expect their loans to be repaid, building owners who have a good, safe building that you rent, outside contractors, are all team relationships. Where on the team can you fit in and help the team be better? Where can you build the team up with your talents?

You cannot fix everything. I have tried to help everyone, and I was stressing myself out. It has taken me a long time to figure out when to say no, how to say no, understand I can't help, or to stop helping someone. You are amazing, and people need your help. Maybe you have a hard time asking for help. It takes practice. It takes practice knowing how to ask for help and when to ask, but it also takes you knowing yourself and being strong enough to ask for help and to say no when you are getting overwhelmed. People need you, but there are times when you have to step back. Overloading yourself won't make you the best teammate.

Give back to your community by training others. Be the coach for people that you wish you had. Be the trainer that you should have had. We had a Colonel talk to us at Officer Candidate School (OCS). He talked about his struggle to get to where he was. He told us if we didn't have a mentor, he would be one for us. He would also try to find us one, but he wanted us to know that he would support us no matter what gender or color we were. He was going to be the mentor he didn't have. You don't need a degree or a title to be a mentor, coach, or teacher, just help other people.

Being a team player will increase your network in a positive way. Maybe one day the company goes bankrupt. Do you want to be the person who never shared credit when he should have? Or would you rather be the person that people think of and say, "Yes, I remember Shawn. He was nice; he gave me credit for my idea and worked hard for that mean guy. Let's hire him to work here."

Have you ever seen someone get promoted, and now they know everything? They hang out with the bosses and won't talk to you? They don't need the team because they are in charge? If you don't like that, then learn from that bad example and don't act that way. There are different ways to learn, and sometimes using bad examples can just be as effective as good examples as long as we choose to learn.

Say hello to the people around you. I was watching a documentary on Warren Buffet, and he got a drink from someone, and he said thank you, asked them their name, and had a conversation with the person. Keep being a human being. If you are the CEO or owner of a billion-dollar company, lots of people will want your time and attention. Sometimes being humble is just saying hi and it goes a long way. When someone walks in the room, and you are in a conversation with someone else, remember that you can still nod your head or smile to acknowledge the new person's presence. Perhaps you and a friend applied for the same job, you got promoted, and he didn't. He might be happy for you, but he will still feel down that he didn't get the job. Don't downplay what you earned, but it will be bittersweet for him. Take him out for a beer, coffee, tea, or have him over for dinner. Show him you still care by your actions. Talk can be cheap.

Critique yourself often. Allow for it. Ask for it. Encourage it. Possibly demand it. It can be difficult to accept someone criticizing you on your project that you have spent hours, days, weeks, months, possibly years on. There were many stories during the pandemic that normal business models weren't working. People could get mad at a person making a suggestion. Businesses that survived after Amazon, Walmart, or other companies moved into their space were ones that adjusted. Maybe you are perfect and have all the ideas, but will you accept ideas/suggestions from your team? If someone criticizes your plan, can you still respond softly? Maybe the situation is intense, a short timeframe, or the person reacted too strongly – don't think too much about the presentation of their idea but what they are trying to say. It can be hard to have someone criticize you or your idea, but it might be worth considering.

When I am hanging a white board in a classroom, I need a plan. I need to make sure it's in the right place with consideration for the projector, so I'll need to talk to IT. I'll consider the lighting in the classroom, and connect with the teacher about various other classroom functions. I'll use a level, measuring tape, the correct screws, and likely help to hang a 300 pound magnetic 8ftx4ft board. Do I get mad when IT has a suggestion or requirement? What about arguing with the teacher? She is the one that needs to use it, so her input is vital. If I need people to talk to or to help me hang the board, I need to coordinate with their schedules. The different tools I need will make it look the best it can. Maybe the building has shifted or the previous board was hung crooked and I possibly need to patch and paint the wall. People on my team can help me level out my plans when there is something I didn't see or know about. What if I'm building a million-dollar building? Wouldn't it be good to talk to the contractor, architect, and the municipality about what was there before? I would probably also need to connect with the department of water and power, accountant, bank for the loan, realtor, and maybe some other people. If I create an environment where people are afraid for their jobs or just a toxic environment in general, if they ask questions or "criticize" the plan, then the final product won't be as good as it can be.

Thank people for giving feedback, a critique, review, or follow-up. It can be difficult to properly critique something or someone – it takes courage. You can thank them for helping you even if you don't adjust, agree, or do their suggestion.

Others

Critique is important, but if you're a leader, you also want to have tact with what you choose to critique and when. Am I criticizing to help them grow or to point out all the stuff they missed? It is easy to criticize someone. We have all met someone who just wants to point out all the things wrong with an idea or plan. They don't offer solutions or offer to help. Sometimes all we see is what is possibly wrong, and we don't know the solution. Maybe the solution is not executing the plan. Work to build them up. Maybe you have a personnel issue with the person. If doing the right thing is helping them succeed, then offer a good critique of their plan. Maybe just point out the biggest issue if their plan is horrible, but always give scaffolding for improvement. The best leaders mentor everyone. Stay neutral. If you don't like them or they don't like you, work on the relationship but don't just disregard their idea because of something personal. You have value. They have value. Just like you want your plan to be the best and succeed. What about others? Do they deserve your best critique or opinion, or are you the leader that only does their best when everything is perfect or only when it's your best friend?

Can you be the greatest? Can you lead? Sure you can! Take the chance and give your voice when people are planning. Create the greatest company, the best product, and win that election. Just don't forget to thank the people who got you there. When you talk, remember to give credit to the team. Kareem Abdul-Jabbar said, "One man can be crucial ingredient on a team, but one man cannot make a team." No matter how hard you train, you need a team. That's okay. Go be the greatest; just don't talk about yourself all the time. There are times to advertise your great company, sports team, or yourself. Train hard, watch and study your competition, use your team to help you be the best you can be, be a part of the team, and help other people become their greatest. Find the balance that works for you. If you don't forget your team, you will probably find the right balance.

Points for reflections:

What are conventional and unconventional ways to grow?

Are you promoting others to take new or different training classes, or are you the one always taking those slots?

Are people seeing authentic humility, or are we boasting of what we have done to make ourselves look better?

Chapter 7
Follow

"A good leader sets the example for others to follow." – US Admiral William McRaven

We've covered what leadership looks like. However, in order to be a good leader, you sometimes have to be a good follower, too. Be a good teammate. One person can't do everything on their own. The world is too big, and there are too many people to help. A leader will find his place on the team to make it better. He is not the one always giving orders. What are some good examples you can think of where the person who was a part of the team was instrumental in helping the "king" succeed?

How about a Broadway show? There's an orchestra, orchestra director, instrument repair people, lead actor, other actors, script writer, musical director, the director for the whole show, stage crew, building maintenance, janitorial staff, ticket people, security, makeup artists, outside contractors, (to replace a window when one of the actor's kids throws a ball) and many others. Everyone must do their job in order for the show to be successful.

I've worked with the maintenance staff at a school that has won awards in Arts, Robotics, Musicals, Football, Soccer, Basketball,

Baseball, Softball, Science Fair projects, and other fun things. Do I get a cool plaque? Does the janitor get a bouquet of flowers at the end of the show? Things get tense, and there is sometimes yelling. If the maintenance team hasn't done their job and made sure the exits are cleared and working right, then others can't do their job right. I knew that my work mattered, even if others didn't notice it. (They would have noticed if the work was done wrong though!) Everyone is a leader of themselves. You decide what you are going to do. Be humble and be on the team to help the team succeed. Is it nice getting a trophy? Yes. But sometimes, and for long periods of time during your lifetime, you'll need to take joy in seeing other people succeed. Take personal responsibility for being the teammate that gets tasks done without being asked. Lead yourself while on a team.

You hear stories of people starting from the bottom and working up through the ranks or levels of the company and becoming the CEO or something else. There are those stories out there, but there are only so many CEOs or other top positions. You can have success being the number 2, or whatever rank you have. My friend commented that she had a good life. She was a secretary at a school and her husband was an administrator at a school and they got the summer off to do whatever they wanted. It allowed her to teach Vacation Bible School (VBS), vacation in Hawaii every two years, own a nice house, and eat out often. She had a nice new car and was happy. She and her husband didn't settle. They worked hard and supported other people. Without her, the school wouldn't have run correctly. Did the principal make her feel valued? Yes, but that's not what drove her. She wanted to do a good job no matter the pay or the title she had or if she got praise from others. She took personal responsibility for her actions and looked for opportunities to do her job well.

One time, there was an event at the school and my whole team was working on various tasks. I heard a call come through that there was a plumbing issue in one of the restrooms. While this wasn't exactly my responsibility, I jumped in. I was responsible for my team and the overall success, so that night, it meant jumping in where I was needed. This is leadership. Do you think I wanted to handle the bathroom issue? Of course I would have rather been the guy at the barbecue, or chatting with students' parents but the reality is that a leader isn't always doing the fun stuff. Have I been put down for being the guy that unclogs a toilet? Yep. But good leaders don't let that get them down.

What am I to do if the person in charge of me is a bad leader or bad person? Some bosses are abusive, jerks, sexist, or racist. Speak out appropriately about it. Use Human Resources or whatever systems you have to solve the problem. Sometimes it won't be solved—document the behavior to protect yourself. My friend was being harassed by his boss for being in the military. He wrote everything down. He still did what his boss said. He still worked hard, showed up on time, was cheerful, was honest, stood up for others, and followed his boss's instructions. After a certain amount of time and not getting promoted because he was in the military, he turned the documentation in. He was promoted, and he didn't have that guy as a boss anymore. Now that is a good story. How many other stories of harassment are out there that don't end well? While following your boss's instructions is important, you always need to protect yourself. If you've reported misconduct through the appropriate channels, and nothing has changed, you might need to find a new job or make a complaint through city, county, state, or federally.

Remember, even when you're following the orders of a boss, you can lead. You can show your teammates how to work with integrity and excellence. Every interaction is an opportunity to demonstrate leadership regardless of your official role.

Am I balancing my need to lead with what my boss or team needs done?

Are you following with blinders on or where you're looking around for what is needed?

Chapter 8

Personal Management

"Those who are victorious plan effectively and change decisively. They are like a great river that maintains its course but adjusts its flow." – Sun Tzu

Friend: "Spencer, where are your boots?"

Me: "I forgot them."

Friend: " Do you know why you forgot your boots? Because your Mom packed for you."

I was in Virginia for a Navy class, and I forgot my boots. I could have said my Mom didn't pack my stuff; she only helped. That would have been petty and beside the point. I am responsible for myself and my actions. That was the last time she helped me pack.

Personal discipline is essential. Are you at the right place, at the right time, wearing the right stuff? There are lots of ways to develop personal discipline. Going to school helps create self-discipline. You can learn it in other ways as well, like the military, or a job. People often also learn personal discipline when they make a mistake and suffer the consequences. For example, if you were fired for being late to work, it's likely that you wouldn't repeat the mistake at your next job. There are many facets to personal discipline. It takes time to learn when to speak and when not to speak. Just because someone says you can speak freely doesn't mean you can say whatever you are thinking. Be measured. Just because you are in college and "free from your parents" doesn't mean you drink all the time, sleep in and miss class, party, do drugs, and so on. Your grades will be impacted. The company that loaned you money will want it paid back with interest. Time will be lost. You can lose everything you have by making one bad choice. Self-control is important.

Some parents require their kids to complete chores. This helps one develop self-control and determination. For those of us who had required chores, we learned discipline and time management. If we had a recurring task, we developed how to anticipate and plan for it. If you didn't have this requirement growing up, there are still ways that you can develop these skills. A good leader manages his time so that he can get all his tasks done before they need to be done and sets himself up for success for the next day. We feel the repercussions of this in everyday life. If you fail to do the dishes from dinner, you'll wake up and have to do them. If you don't do them the next morning, your house might start to smell. This effect will likely inspire you to be more proactive with dish washing.

Set yourself up for success by a little planning to make today and tomorrow go as smoothly as possible. Don't overwhelm yourself with planning. If you have a general plan that can get you going in the right direction, that might be just enough. Establishing a flexible routine often inspires people to complete required daily tasks. Try additional adjustments to the routine to see if you have a more productive day. Allow room for things to go wrong and for breaks. (Sometimes a productive day is fitting a nap into your schedule.) You can easily over-commit yourself, and you want to be a successful leader. You can set yourself up for failure by failing to plan, not allowing for the unexpected, or by taking on too much. If you were starting a business, you would think about what you are going to make, how you will make it, sell it, ship it, and so on. The same is true when you're managing yourself. Plan out your time.

Being prompt demonstrates self-discipline. It tells others you can handle your own life and schedule. Showing up early shows people that the event they are putting on is important to you. There are times to be late, but generally, people like it when people show up on time. For example, if you are going to a job interview and you are late, you probably are not going to get the job. Tardiness makes a potential boss question you. Are you reliable? If you are late or late all the time, why would a supervisor hire you or pick you to lead a team? If you can't complete projects on time, why would you expect to be assigned to lead again, if at all? Your team might pick up your bad habit of being late and be late as well. If you can't control your speech or hands, what is the next inappropriate thing you will say or do? That's a liability for the organization and it would make sense for that hiring manager to not offer you a job. Something as simple as being on time can get you a job, or make you lose it.

Fiscal discipline

Spend within your means. A good leader will find ways to help people as efficiently as possible. Remember the story about my mom? She would change out the flowers in the bathrooms at church about every other week. She used fake flowers so she could reuse them. They looked real at first glance, and they were in her budget. My stepmom is a fantastic cook. She's known for her simple and inexpensive meals that are delicious and healthy. She didn't always go to expensive stores. She shopped around, used coupons, and the refrigerator was always packed with good food. Did we go out to eat every once in a while? Yes, but it was budgeted for.

The community around you needs help. That might be your church, your family, or people you don't know. My mom and stepmom helped their community in tangible ways. What are ways that you can give to your community? It's important to give to charities and organizations that can help those in need. Giving a couple of bucks here and there is not giving enough—budget a responsible amount. I give more than 10%. Is it a stretch? Sometimes, but am I shopping around, buying on sale, eating in, not buying everything I want, but everything I need. I am not miserable. I have a roof over my head. If I spend selfishly or extravagantly, is that an example of a leader? My community needs my support just like yours does. There is a balance of supporting your community with your spending and your charity. If you live in a place that is well off, then find somewhere else to give. Spend some time and effort to make your donation count. You need to find your own balance on how much you give, but don't ask me why there are issues in your community when you only give a couple of bucks. Are there scams? Yes, so give to established groups. Charities need you to volunteer time, but they also need your financial support. Maybe you need to be charitable at work. Maybe buying a couple of coffees or lunch is a good idea. I remember when my mom died, people were buying me lunch to spend time with me. That was a help for me. There are different ways to lead.

Prove that you can be responsible for the financial well being of a company by proving you can be responsible for your own finances. Paying your bills and saving for emergencies is important. Save for retirement. Save for...everything! This will help you have money for the unexpected bill. Having savings will help you have money so that when your co-worker's house is washed away in a flood, you have the ability to help them. Need a new car? Well, saving a little bit every month will help you have some money set aside for the purchase. Maybe the unexpected is a recession or pandemic. Flat tires happen. Medical emergencies happen. There are plenty of articles and books about different ways to save, so do some research and figure out what works best for you. Like charity, giving a couple of bucks and saving a couple of bucks is okay to start with, but to be effective, it needs to be substantial. Paying your bills on time is cheaper than having a late fee. People don't trust others who are always late on their bills. Leaders build trust with what they say and what they do. Why would I get promoted if my car is getting repossessed for not paying my bills? How am I going to be trusted to manage a budget?

I don't know if I have ever seen someone lead effectively and have bad money management. It doesn't mean you will or won't be rich, but living within your means while giving helps your community.

Bribes

Bribes and other illegal/unethical methods to increase your income are something we don't talk about very much. They are wrong. Can you make more money by personally paying someone to win the contract? Yes. Can you get kickbacks by charging more and approving someone's bid? Yes. If you don't claim everything on your taxes that you are supposed to, then you can buy something cool. You could falsely add time to your timecard. Various ways to get ahead will be all around you, but if you're a leader, you'll act with integrity. It speaks to your character whether or not you take or offer a bribe.

Be organized

You are called upon to make various decisions throughout the day. Having fewer things to think or worry about is helpful. Reducing the distractions or background noise will help you think.

I have read countless articles about having a daily, weekly, or monthly plan or schedule. At basic training for the military, you have to pack your stuff a certain way. One night I let someone borrow my flashlight, but shortly after I needed to find my socks. It was dark, but my area was organized properly; I stuck my hand in the area where I thought the socks were, and they were there. I didn't have to wake anyone up or spend extra time searching for them. Spending a little time organizing myself saved me aggravation later. Being organized will also help you not overcommit yourself as you have organized your time. Overcommitting yourself can lead you to being overwhelmed, stressed out, and rushed. When someone comes to you asking for help, maybe you aren't as nice to them as you could have been.

Managing yourself includes managing your time, commitments, and finances. Being a great leader in your personal life will allow you to be a great leader in your professional life.

What planning, organization, clearing out, managing do you need to work on to be more productive, able to find that thing, or more relaxed?

Are you trying different organization or planning styles from other people to see if you can use their input?

Is your budget where it needs to be for you and your family/ community?

Chapter 9

Discipline

"Be a yardstick of quality. Some people aren't used to an environment where excellence is expected." – Steve Jobs

We've covered personal discipline, but when you're a leader, you have to encourage others to be disciplined as well. It is a part of mentoring others. There are standards in place to ensure that things run properly. Precision matters in many circumstances. Keys have to be precise. Locks and latches and other security-related items have to be aligned properly, or they won't work. Discipline is the same thing. You, your organization, your company, your family, and your city all have rules and regulations they go by, and as a leader, you need to enforce them.

Crushing

You have to do it. You have to hold people accountable. If you are in charge or not, you have to hold yourself and others to the standard. There are various ways to do it. You can hold people to a standard no matter what your position is. If you are not in charge, are you not going to tell someone to stop stealing? It can be intimidating to discipline someone or tell them to stop. But people who walk in integrity encourage others to be better. Even with a multitude of examples, I have a hard time thinking of when discipline was perfect. One size doesn't fit all, and generally, you and I want to be perfect. Do not let the perfect be the enemy of good. Do something. If you see someone do something wrong, pull them aside and talk to them. There will be time for group training later. Don't embarrass people. Look them in the eye and ask questions, talk to them, explain what the issue is and why it cannot be repeated. Maybe you have only seen people yell for discipline, and you don't want to do that, but the dude making that sexually suggestive comment again is just making you mad. Maybe you weren't perfect before you were in charge, and now you have to tell your friends who you are now in charge of to knock it off. Maybe you need to forgive yourself and move on. Like most things in life, you will get better with experience. Leadership is a difficult thing to master; discipline is an area of leadership that is hard to master, and you will get better with time. It's not a good thing to have more opportunities to discipline people as it can wear on you, but you will get a better understanding of situations, ask better questions about what happened, and be more careful with your words in explaining how to make better choices next time.

During World War 2, General Patton was visiting wounded troops in the hospital. There was a soldier there who he thought wasn't hurt. The soldier had no outside appearance of a wound. He talked to the soldier and eventually slapped the soldier. His chain of command reprimanded him (a written statement saying he did something wrong) and told him to apologize to the soldier and to his entire unit or be fired. He apologized to the soldier and the unit as a whole. You might want to handle the situation differently. Don't be afraid to ask for advice. Discipline is a tricky thing, but you have to do it. People will still respect you after you discipline them, or they need to grow up. Letting people get away with bad behavior can lead to a toxic environment where a little here and a little there grows into bigger things down the road. Being consistent is key. Maybe you are the only one disciplining. That's okay. Consider the way you discipline. Some people yell and cuss to reprimand, but that's not always the best tactic. Focus on how you like to be talked to and remember that you are doing great and making the world a better place.

Don't rush to crush

There is a time and place to not criticize everything. Maybe people are tired. Maybe the late person is only a minute late today. Don't pick at people. Maybe you are tired, and you should discipline people tomorrow. There are some things that need an immediate reaction, and some things can wait. So keep it timely. If you wait too long you can still mentor them but if you bring something up after a long period of time it will create an environment of uncertainty.

There are things that you cannot overlook. This also means you don't need to walk around all day pointing out people's mistakes. Handle things in your area. Ask your mentor about it. Discipline isn't a one-size-fits-all, but there are many ways different past experiences will help you make a decision for the issue today. Study different ways people have conducted discipline.

Be gentle. Sometimes it's humbling, scary, depressing, humiliating, or disappointing to mess up and have someone correct you. Think about it. When you do something wrong, and someone calls you out, how do you feel? Maybe you feel ashamed. This isn't a fun feeling, but hopefully the person calling us out has our best interest in mind. There is a time and place to be gentle. Talk to them. Whatever the issue is, make sure it is clear. Come alongside them and be there with them. Teach them the right way. I led a team project that involved painting. After we finished painting, I asked one of my team members to clean the paint rollers and if he knew how to clean them since he was new. He said he knew how to do it. I briefly went to check on another room and when I came back, he was already done cleaning the rollers. I asked him how he cleaned them so quickly and he said, "I got the hose and" I said "Stop. Don't say anything else. This is how I want you to clean rollers in the future." I explained how to clean the paint rollers. In this exchange, I not only taught him something new, but also invested in our relationship and to stop him from doing something wrong. I took the time to correct his behavior in a firm, but kind way. Remember what it feels like to screw up? I was at Boy Scout camp, and a bunch of us got yelled at for doing something dumb. I was not offended by the yelling, but my Scoutmaster knew his audience.

One time, I was at a football game, and a player did something wrong; the coach cussed at him and told the player that he would never play again because of his mistake. I thought the coach went overboard, but I wasn't in charge; so it wasn't my call. Two drunk dads on the sidelines and I spent the next 10 minutes trying to encourage the kid not to quit, as there was a lot of time left in the game, and there would be another game. You will have to make a judgment call. You have to be mature enough to know your tendencies. If you get angry and rage, maybe you need to take a minute to calm down before responding.

Somebody does something wrong. It might be one of those many, many times in your life where it's dumb enough to be a good story later. Don't tell the "funny story" to your spouse on the phone in the lunchroom. There will be time later to laugh about it in private. Protect your people. See the action, correct the action, provide opportunities for growth and encouragement and move on. Don't let them hang their head and let people whisper and gossip about them. Conduct discipline, but protect your people. Grow just like we want to grow ourselves.

Friend- Ross.

Me- Yes.

Friend- I don't want to do this.

Me- Why?

Friend- Because…

Me- Why?

Friend- Silence

Me- Because you don't want them giving you a hard time because you are a girl?

Friend- Yes.

I had a friend confide in me that she didn't want to do something because she didn't want others to give her a hard time for being a girl. Regardless of your gender, age, or whatever if you need to manage people: Get it done. You will have people work against you. We have made mistakes before. Being a leader requires you to discipline people. You have to do it. You have to discipline, correct, and/or stop people from continuing the bad actions. Sometimes it's something simple, and you just need to talk to them; sometimes it's very difficult, and someone has to go to jail. There are many different issues and outcomes. But a good leader has to act. Maybe you are the only employee that is holding people to account. Maybe you have become an unpopular boss because you hold people to the line. There was a poster up in the Azusa National Guard Armory that stated: "Don't create a new standard by not disciplining the people around you." It's hard to discipline your friends, but it is easy to mentor them. Maybe think of it as a way to mentor them to be successful in their future. Even if you don't like the person, take the time to not just walk by them and point out the error, but help them get to the right answer. Let's help the broken people. If someone does something wrong and they get crushed so bad, they might lose motivation and hope. If all you do is point out that they did something wrong, gossip about it, remind them of it constantly, don't allow them to grow, and/or don't mentor them, then you're not leading.

Maybe you've made mistakes; remember that you learned from it and have grown and understood it was wrong. Don't let bad behavior continue because you used to do it. Be the correct example today. It will take time to build credibility, but it can be done.

What are the values that you live by, and are you holding yourself and other people to account?

Looking back, what should someone have disciplined you on so you could be better? How can that apply today?

In your discipline, are you asking questions and being curious about the entire story or just waiting to crush people?

So, can you lead?

Yes. We all need your help, good ideas, and voice. You work hard. You want to help others by creating jobs, volunteering your time to get something done or be a better spouse or parent or family member. You keep learning. You keep trying to grow from the people you interact with, books you read, and different life experiences you have. You have a commitment and the right attitude. There are a lot of quotes and news articles that you are using to grow. Your creativity in helping the team solve the problem speaks to your good initiative. You value and give credit to the work of others. You have found a way to maximize your time, talent, and treasure for the benefit of your community. You stand up for others. You can lead. You do lead.

This book is dedicated to Dad, Mom, and my stepmom.

Special thanks to
Dana Croxton for letting me share a part of his story. You can connect with him at
dana@enableministries.com or
2369 Royal Ave. Simi Valley, CA 93065

To the multiple people who helped proofread, give advice and encouragement.

www.ingramcontent.com/pod-product-compliance
Lightning Source LLC
LaVergne TN
LVHW052104160826
845678LV00015B/3348
9798985989106